TO:

Erin

FROM:

Shen

DATE:

2021

I have been a *huge* fan of Lindsey Bonnice for years now. Her whimsical world of fluffy farm animals is so inspiring. I love her photography, and as a fellow adoptive mama, I am proud to call her a friend. Thank you, Lindsey, for all the positive energy you bring into our lives!

ELSIE LARSON, coauthor of *A Beautiful Mess*

Such a beautiful and uplifting book filled with photos that will leave you smiling from ear to ear and make your heart skip a beat!

ROXANNE WEST, *Bonjour Bliss Blog*

This delightful book is full of sweetness and pawsitivity. Lindsey's love of all things soft and pastel, along with her strong desire to add joy, hope, and encouragement to people's lives, make this book a must-have. And the pictures—oh, the pictures! The fluffy babies are sure to brighten your day and make your heart smile.

SANDI SWIRIDOFF, author of *Reagandoodle & Little Buddy*, reagandoodle.com

Guaranteed, *The Sweet Fluff* will make even the most serious characters smile! Lindsey's signature style is splashed all over the pages, and her generous heart overflows into the words and verse selections she has chosen to share. A talented photographer, gifted businesswoman, and loving wife and mom, Lindsey brings joy through a simple and clear message. Inspiring and uplifting, Lindsey's book will be a treasure to keep and to give for years to come.

VICTORIA DUERSTOCK, speaker and award-winning author of multiple books, including the Heart & Home books, *Extraordinary Hospitality for Ordinary Christians*, and *Advent Devotions & Christmas Crafts for Families*

The Sweet Fluff is exactly what the world needs. Both uplifting and inspiring, the imagery and quotes are sure to bring smiles to faces of all ages. Lindsey's positive and motivational outlook offers an endearing approach to the little (and big) things in life.

AMY TANGERINE, author of *Craft a Life You Love*

Completely enchanting! If you love cute animals as our family does, this book needs to be on your coffee table. *The Sweet Fluff* is a heartwarming, candy-colored escape, and I loved looking through it with my kids! Lindsey's gorgeous photographs of lovable creatures, paired with uplifting quotes and Scripture verses, will absolutely fill your eyes and heart with joy. It's the perfect gift! Pure sweetness.

SHERRI BEMIS, singer-songwriter in the band Eisley

the sweet fluff

the sweet fluff

CUDDLY ANIMALS & INSPIRATIONAL
THOUGHTS FOR A JOYFUL HEART

LINDSEY BONNICE
Creator of *Live* SWEET

TYNDALE
MOMENTUM®

The Tyndale nonfiction imprint

Visit Tyndale online at tyndale.com.

Visit Tyndale Momentum online at tyndalemomentum.com.

TYNDALE, Tyndale's quill logo, *Tyndale Momentum*, and the Tyndale Momentum logo are registered trademarks of Tyndale House Ministries. Tyndale Momentum is the nonfiction imprint of Tyndale House Publishers, Carol Stream, Illinois.

The Sweet Fluff: Cuddly Animals and Inspirational Thoughts for a Joyful Heart

Designed by Lindsey Bergsma

Published in association with the literary agency of C.Y.L.E. Literary Agency, P.O. Box 1, Clarklake, MI 49234.

For information about special discounts for bulk purchases, please contact Tyndale House Publishers at csresponse@tyndale.com, or call 1-800-323-9400.

ISBN 978-1-4964-4940-5

Printed in China

27	26	25	24	23	22	21
7	6	5	4	3	2	1

Dedication

TO MY SWEET BABIES, Noah, Libby, Finn, and Claire: Being a mom was always my biggest dream, and you made that dream come true. You are all so funny, happy, and silly in your own unique ways, and I love getting to be your mama more than anything! You are my biggest blessings, and you bring so much joy to our home and to everyone who has the honor of knowing you. I love you more than words can express!

Introduction

I DREAMED OF BEING A PHOTOGRAPHER from the time I was a little girl. Finding things to take pictures of was pretty easy: My family had cats, dogs, and bunnies that I cherished, and I enjoyed capturing them on film. What a perfect pairing of my passions!

When I was a teenager, a dear friend's sheep gave birth to triplet lambs. The mama sheep abandoned one of them, and my friend asked whether I would take care of the lamb. Rescue a sweet, fluffy animal baby? Absolutely! With my parents' permission, Posey lived in our house and slept next to my bed. I bottle-fed her every three hours. That's when my love for farming was sparked!

In the following years, my parents added goats and chickens and more lambs to our little family farm.

I adored all of them, and photographing them brought me so much joy. I spent hours creating scrapbooks and hanging pictures of my animal friends on my bedroom walls.

Fast-forward to today. I live with my husband and our four sweet children on a small hobby farm located on the same lake I grew up on. I am inspired by so many things around me; rarely a day goes by without my kiddos and our fluffy loves being caught on camera in a photograph or video.

My pets have brought so much happiness to my life. I hope that these images and the accompanying words do the same for you, making you smile and bringing you an extra bit of joy!

XO

Lindsey Bonnice

What brings you joy? Give yourself an extra helping today.

LINDSEY

Shout to the LORD, all the
earth; break out in praise and
sing for joy! . . . Let the earth
and all living things join in.

PSALM 98:4, 7

You have the power to brighten other people's lives with your words and actions.

LINDSEY

How wonderful
it is that no
one has to wait,
but can start
right now to
gradually change
the world!

ANNE FRANK

I praise you, for I am

fearfully and wonderfully made.

PSALM 139:14, ESV

Hug tighter,
smile bigger,
love harder, and
offer forgiveness
without hesitation.

LINDSEY

Don't worry about tomorrow,

for tomorrow will bring its

own worries. Today's trouble

is enough for today.

MATTHEW 6:34

Let love flow
from you
without
expectation.

LINDSEY

"I know the plans I have for you," says the LORD. "They are plans for good and not for disaster, to give you a future and a hope. In those days when you pray, I will listen. If you look for me wholeheartedly, you will find me."

JEREMIAH 29:11-13

Friends are the sunshine of life.

JOHN HAY

Hug someone
today with your
entire being.

LINDSEY

Let's not get tired
of doing what is good.
At just the right time we will
reap a harvest of blessing
if we don't give up.

GALATIANS 6:9

Wonder . . . is the basis of worship.

THOMAS CARLYLE

sweet thoughts

People often ask, "Why do you have so many animals?" Since childhood, I have always had a special love for fluffy, furry, feathered friends. I was the little girl who asked for a kitten or puppy or duckling for each birthday, Christmas, and Easter! Now as an adult, so many of my animal dreams have come true with a farm full of fluffy, and also bristly, loves!

Animals calm me when I'm anxious or frazzled, and that special connection helps me to slow down and soak up the beauty in life. I am always working on projects and creating while my mind is going a mile a minute. My pets have been the perfect reminder to not run so fast and miss all the blessings around me.

Isn't it wonderful that God created animals to be such sweet companions for us? When we're having an especially hard day and our energy is depleted, their unconditional love can fill us back up. So much of my stress and exhaustion slips away when one of my donkeys nuzzles me in the barnyard, or when my piggy begs for a belly rub, or when my sweet little pup Winnie hops up on my lap and wants nothing more than my presence.

To me, pets are a beautiful representation of how much God loves us. These wonderful animals never fail to bring extra moments of joy.

> O LORD, what a variety of things you
> have made! In wisdom you have made them
> all. The earth is full of your creatures. . . . May
> the glory of the LORD continue forever! The
> LORD takes pleasure in all he has made!
>
> PSALM 104:24, 31

Life is difficult on many days, but God always comforts us.

LINDSEY

God blesses those

who patiently endure

testing and temptation.

Afterward they will

receive the crown of life

that God has promised

to those who love him.

JAMES 1:12

Extend grace
to others often,
and to yourself
even more.

LINDSEY

37

I will lift up the cup of

salvation and praise the LORD's

name for saving me.

PSALM 116:13

Love each
other dearly
always. There
is scarcely
anything else
in the world
but that: to love
one another.

JEAN VALJEAN IN
LES MISÉRABLES

Come to me, all of you

who are weary and

carry heavy burdens,

and I will give you rest.

Take my yoke upon you.

Let me teach you,

because I am humble and

gentle at heart, and you

will find rest for your souls.

MATTHEW 11:28-29

Always try to
end the day with a
beautiful thought
or memory to
add sweetness to
your dreams.

LINDSEY

The purpose of my instruction

is that all believers would

be filled with love that comes

from a pure heart, a clear

conscience, and genuine faith.

1 TIMOTHY 1:5

Don't judge each day by the harvest you reap but by the seeds you plant.

ATTRIBUTED TO
ROBERT LOUIS STEVENSON

Your unfailing love is better

than life itself; how I praise you!

PSALM 63:3

See the glitter
in every day,
and welcome these
glints of God's
goodness.

LINDSEY

No power in the sky
above or in the earth
below—indeed, nothing
in all creation will
ever be able to separate
us from the love of
God that is revealed in
Christ Jesus our Lord.

ROMANS 8:39

If the world seems
cold to you, kindle
fires to warm it!

LUCY LARCOM

sweet thoughts

Last year, a dear friend of mine told me about a new routine she had started with her grown daughter. The daughter had just delivered her first baby, and it was a difficult birth that took a physical and emotional toll on her. She and her mother were trying to keep each other's spirits up, so they started going on gratitude walks to remember just how blessed they were, despite the hardships they were facing. Once a week, they would get together and walk, taking turns sharing aloud something they were thankful for.

I was so intrigued with their idea that I decided to try it with my children. Oh my word—what a blessing it's been for us! The children have been eager participants. As I expected, they thanked God for Mommy and Daddy and their grandparents and friends. But then they expressed gratitude for specific outings and special times together too. I'm amazed that such an effortless activity can be so life changing, even for young children.

When you declare aloud the things you are thankful for and hear others doing the same, your attitude is transformed and you're filled with such joy! I think it's the perfect way to pick yourself up, and others too. After all, a grateful heart is a full heart!

Let them praise the LORD for
his great love and for the wonderful
things he has done for them. Let them
offer sacrifices of thanksgiving and sing
joyfully about his glorious acts.

PSALM 107:21-22

Never underestimate the happiness that simple thoughtfulness can bring.

LINDSEY

Let all who take refuge

in you rejoice; let them

ever sing for joy, and spread

your protection over them,

that those who love your

name may exult in you.

For you bless the righteous,

O LORD; you cover him with

favor as with a shield.

PSALM 5:11-12, ESV

One of the first signs
of a Spirit-filled
life is enthusiasm!

ATTRIBUTED TO
A. B. SIMPSON

God said . . . "When I see
the rainbow in the clouds, I will
remember the eternal covenant
between God and every living
creature on earth."

GENESIS 9:12, 16

When you
choose to have a
grateful heart, the
world becomes even
more beautiful.

LINDSEY

You make known to me
the path of life; in your
presence there is fullness
of joy; at your right hand are
pleasures forevermore.

PSALM 16:11, ESV

The great use of a life
is to spend it for some-
thing that outlasts it.

WILLIAM JAMES

Always pray and
never give up.

LUKE 18:1

Crazy hair;
don't care.
Smile anyway.

LINDSEY

The LORD delights in his people;

he crowns the humble with victory.

PSALM 149:4

To err
is human;
to forgive,
divine.

ALEXANDER POPE

This is my command—
be strong and courageous!
Do not be afraid or discouraged.
For the LORD your God is
with you wherever you go.

JOSHUA 1:9

sweet thoughts

Have you ever experienced someone saying something kind to you out of the blue, offering a little surprise compliment that really turned your mood around? I know I have, and I am so thankful for the people who have poured their kind words into my life.

Oftentimes I think sweet thoughts about someone, but I'm too shy to say the words out loud, send them in a text, or post them in a comment. Several women have entered my life in recent years who are amazing at lifting up others and me with their encouraging words, and their examples have inspired me to be more intentional about trying the same.

I am keenly aware about what comes out of my mouth. We all know how much it hurts when someone says something harsh to us; it's like an arrow piercing our hearts. So I try very hard to stop and think before I speak. Many times when I am worn out or stressed, I react unkindly; but more and more, I've discovered the impact of offering others heartfelt blessings.

At first it may feel awkward to give someone an unexpected compliment, yet the truth is that our kind, loving words can be an amazing gift! It doesn't have to be a huge gesture. What if we intentionally made a point to tell friends how much they mean to us, thanked others when they lend us help, or let our family members know what a good job they're doing?

God has shown me that I can share his love each and every day through a simple text, a phone call, a comment on social media, or by taking a moment to thank the people in my life for the ways they've blessed me! We all can make a difference every day!

Kind words are like honey—sweet
to the soul and healthy for the body.

PROVERBS 16:24

Throw compliments around like confetti. No cleanup required.

LINDSEY

Whatever is good and
perfect is a gift coming
down to us from God our
Father, who created all
the lights in the heavens.
He never changes or
casts a shifting shadow.

JAMES 1:17

The power of
finding beauty
in the humblest
things makes
home happy
and life lovely.

LOUISA MAY ALCOTT

I will sing to

the LORD because he

is good to me.

PSALM 13:6

Scatter laughter

like sprinkles

on a cupcake.

LINDSEY

This is real love—not that
we loved God, but that he loved
us and sent his Son as a sacrifice
to take away our sins.

1 JOHN 4:10

[God] must be present in every single creature in its innermost and outermost being, on all sides, through and through . . . so that nothing can be more truly present and within all creatures than God himself with his power.

MARTIN LUTHER

Anyone who belongs to Christ

has become a new person. The old

life is gone; a new life has begun!

2 CORINTHIANS 5:17

Find joy in the
little things in life,
like puppy kisses
and chocolate bars.

LINDSEY

Taste and see

that the LORD

is good.

Oh, the joys

of those who

take refuge in him!

PSALM 34:8

No legacy is so rich as honesty.

WILLIAM SHAKESPEARE

Do nothing from selfish ambition

or conceit, but in humility

count others more significant

than yourselves.

PHILIPPIANS 2:3, ESV

sweet thoughts

For years I had wanted to design a line of children's products, but I wondered whether I had the talent to make it happen. Would I be able to figure out how to create products? And if I did, would anyone like them enough to buy them?

The fear of failing and the fear of change held me back. Has that ever happened to you? This double-edged fear can prevent us from starting projects, from chasing our dreams, from trying new things. I jotted down changes I wanted to implement and ideas I wanted to try, and I spent countless hours studying them by reading, listening to podcasts, and watching seminars. But I never actually ended up taking any action.

Then I remembered something I had heard years before, and it changed my outlook: A woman had said it was better to start something when it's not quite the perfect time than to wait until the perfect time and possibly never start at all.

That advice was a game changer for me since I often put things off until it's the right time. It was true: I was waiting for a better season of life when I had more time. But then I realized this was wishful thinking and that now was as good as ever! I needed to quit nitpicking, stop questioning, and just take the leap to begin.

Here's my challenge to you: Get started! Make a list of things you'd like to attempt or accomplish, pick just one, and then take the necessary steps to put it into action! You'll be amazed how far you can go.

Work brings profit, but
mere talk leads to poverty!

PROVERBS 14:23

Celebrate &
choose to be
present each day,
because every day
is truly a gift!

LINDSEY

Jesus Christ

is the same

yesterday,

today,

and forever.

HEBREWS 13:8

Everything that is done in the world is done by hope.

MARTIN LUTHER

Trust in the LORD with all
your heart, and do not lean on
your own understanding. In all your
ways acknowledge him, and he
will make straight your paths.

PROVERBS 3:5-6, ESV

I'm a hugger.
Want to join me?

LINDSEY

I can do everything through Christ,

who gives me strength.

PHILIPPIANS 4:13

Give thanks,
for unknown
blessings are
already on
their way.

NATIVE AMERICAN
SAYING

I pray that your hearts
will be flooded with
light so that you can
understand the confident
hope [God] has given to
those he called—his holy
people who are his rich
and glorious inheritance.

EPHESIANS 1:18

You can never
get enough hogs
and kisses.

LINDSEY

May the grace of
the Lord Jesus be with
God's holy people.

REVELATION 22:21

Patience
is bitter,
but its fruit
is sweet.

JOHN CHARDIN

How good and pleasant

it is when God's people

live together in unity!

PSALM 133:1, NIV

sweet thoughts

Through the years I've struggled with anxious thoughts and worry. When these thoughts take over, they affect not only my mood but my choices as well. But as I've grown closer to God through his Word and prayer, I've realized I can take control of how I think and feel. Instead of focusing on the negative, I can intentionally choose to see God's blessings and his grace in my life.

This deliberate change in perspective brightens each day, even when the actual circumstances I'm in haven't changed. I can be grateful for what I've learned instead of obsessive about my failure. Even when I temporarily miss out on doing something fun with my family because of deadline pressures, I can still appreciate the extra time I've been given to accomplish what I've been working on. I can choose to be joyful for the sweet little memories I made, even when my plans didn't go the way I had hoped.

How are you doing today? Dear friends, God offers us grace each day. If we choose to live presently in that grace and share it with others, our woes can turn into joys, and our anxieties can turn into thankfulness!

It is good to give thanks to the LORD, to sing praises to the Most High. It is good to proclaim your unfailing love in the morning, your faithfulness in the evening. . . . You thrill me, LORD, with all you have done for me!

PSALM 92:1-2, 4

A grateful heart
is a full heart, and
it never tires of
saying thank you.

LINDSEY

Love is patient and kind. Love is

not jealous or boastful or proud.

1 CORINTHIANS 13:4

The story of
Jesus . . . is the
greatest story
in the world, the
greatest romance,
and we are called
to the greatest
adventure.

FATHER RAPHAEL SIMON

I am coming soon.

Hold on to what you have,

so that no one will

take away your crown.

REVELATION 3:11

Take time to
rejoice in both
the big and little
victories in life.

LINDSEY

Ask, and it will be given to you;

seek, and you will find;

knock, and it will be opened to you.

MATTHEW 7:7, ESV

Life is the flower for which love is the honey.

ATTRIBUTED TO
VICTOR HUGO

God is so rich in mercy, and he

loved us so much . . . he gave us life.

EPHESIANS 2:4-5

When life gets overwhelming, focus on the positive, and keep moving forward.

LINDSEY

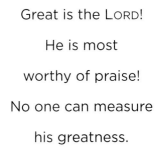

Great is the Lord!

He is most

worthy of praise!

No one can measure

his greatness.

PSALM 145:3

The value of an idea lies in the using of it.

THOMAS A. EDISON

You prepare a feast

for me in the presence

of my enemies.

You honor me by

anointing my head with oil.

My cup overflows

with blessings.

Surely your goodness

and unfailing love

will pursue me

all the days of my life,

and I will live in the house

of the LORD forever.

PSALM 23:5-6

sweet thoughts

Life sometimes sneaks up on us, doesn't it? Our days are filled with jobs, appointments, housework, laundry, and meal preparation. We have to-do lists that keep growing longer before we even realize it, and in some seasons, those unfinished lists feel more overwhelming than at other times.

When this happens to me, I don't panic or frantically try to get more things done. Instead I take a step back and acknowledge that my plate is full with more going on than usual. I take a deep breath and tell myself, "It's okay, Lindsey. This won't last forever."

But the other thing I do may seem counterintuitive: I intentionally put aside my tasks and enjoy the little things, such as snuggling with my favorite fluffy friends, stepping outside into the fresh air, or spending a few more minutes with the people I love.

Doing something that brings me joy and helps clear my head sometimes makes all the difference. It works for me, and I hope you'll consider this suggestion. When we are intentional about making sure we have time to rest and time to work, we all can be much more productive.

Give all your worries and cares to God,
for he cares about you.

1 PETER 5:7

You'll always
stand out
when you're true
to yourself.

LINDSEY

Always be joyful.

Never stop praying.

Be thankful in all circumstances,

for this is God's will for you who

belong to Christ Jesus.

1 THESSALONIANS 5:16-18

When one door
of happiness closes,
another opens; but often
we look so long at the
closed door that we do
not see the one which
has been opened for us.

UNKNOWN

In peace I will

lie down and sleep,

for you alone, O Lᴏʀᴅ,

will keep me safe.

PSALM 4:8

Everyone has
their own specialty.
Don't spend your
whole life trying
to be good at
someone else's.

LINDSEY

Come, let us sing
to the LORD!
Let us shout joyfully
to the Rock
of our salvation.

PSALM 95:1

What you leave behind is not what is engraved in stone monuments, but what is woven into the lives of others.

THUCYDIDES,
PARAPHRASING PERICLES

Binge
on joy,
and gift
others with
the surplus.

LINDSEY

Always be full of joy in the
Lord. I say it again—rejoice!
Let everyone see that you
are considerate in all you do.
Remember, the Lord is
coming soon. Don't worry
about anything; instead, pray
about everything. Tell God
what you need, and thank
him for all he has done.

PHILIPPIANS 4:4-6

A flower cannot blossom without sunshine, and man cannot live without love.

MAX MÜLLER

You make
me smile,
even on
the rainiest
of days!

LINDSEY

Faith is a living, daring confidence in God's grace.

MARTIN LUTHER

Those who trust in the LORD

will find new strength. They will

soar high on wings like eagles.

They will run and not grow weary.

They will walk and not faint.

ISAIAH 40:31

sweet thoughts

We all experience various hardships in our lives, and some of us face more adversity than others. I've been fortunate not to have gone through many tragedies in my life, but I have had my fair share of trials. Sometimes when I was in the thick of them, I felt as if I were being thrown from side to side with no end in sight. Fears and questions kept rushing through my mind, and I couldn't stop crying.

When our daughter Claire had to spend almost a month in the NICU, I asked God why my sweet girl had to suffer so much. His answer came in the outpouring of love from my dear friends and family and thousands of people I'd never met before. There were phone calls with prayers and texts of encouragement to remind me that God had all of it under control. Many afternoons after a difficult day at the hospital, a rainbow would appear in the sky: a sign that God loves us all and that he keeps his promises.

During each of my storms, I leaned into God more than ever. He cradled me in his arms and sent loving people who prayed over me and guided me. He remained constant. When the difficult situation was over, I could look back and honestly say, "Thank you, God, for never leaving my side. I sensed your closeness during those dark days."

Here's what I know: After my storms calmed, I saw beautiful blessings and learned lessons from the struggles, even when the trials ended in heartache. God doesn't let any sorrow go to waste.

Thankfully for us, Claire got through that month in the hospital and now is a happy, active two-year-old.

May you have the power to understand, as all
God's people should, how wide, how long, how
high, and how deep his love is.

EPHESIANS 3:18

Friendships are discovered rather than made.

ATTRIBUTED TO
HARRIET BEECHER STOWE

Life's a party,
and you're invited.
It wouldn't
be as much fun
without you.

LINDSEY

Turn away from evil and
do good. Search for peace,
and work to maintain it.

PSALM 34:14

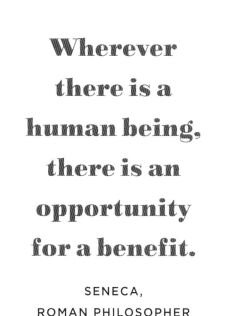

Wherever there is a human being, there is an opportunity for a benefit.

SENECA,
ROMAN PHILOSOPHER

Use your
words to
wrap others
in kindness.

LINDSEY

Let us strip off every weight that slows us down, especially the sin that so easily trips us up. And let us run with endurance the race God has set before us. We do this by keeping our eyes on Jesus, the champion who initiates and perfects our faith.

HEBREWS 12:1-2

Every realm of
nature is marvelous.

ARISTOTLE

Let the world
see your sweetness
in the way you
live each day.

LINDSEY

God has not given us a spirit

of fear and timidity, but of power,

love, and self-discipline.

2 TIMOTHY 1:7

The secret
of getting
ahead
is getting
started.

UNKNOWN

God's miracles
take my breath
away—unexpected
and lavish gifts
from him.

LINDSEY

I will give thanks to the Lᴏʀᴅ

with my whole heart; I will recount

all of your wonderful deeds. I will be

glad and exult in you; I will sing praise

to your name, O Most High.

PSALM 9:1-2, ESV

When your light
shines brightly,
the world sparkles
even more because
you're in it.

LINDSEY

sweet thoughts

I hope you've been inspired, encouraged, and delighted with this collection of photographs, Bible verses, timely quotes, and words expressed from my heart. It has been fun to put it together.

You may have noticed the word *joy* pops up a lot in the book. There was a time in my life when my joy came from reaching the next goal or climbing the ladder a little higher. Having big goals and dreams is awesome, but here's the truth: We can't count on them to bring us lasting joy.

True joy and fulfillment can come only from a personal relationship with the Lord. He is steadfast through all our ups and downs, and his love endures forever, even when our plans fail. He promises to be with us in every stage of our lives—through hardships and celebrations and everything in between.

Sin has separated every one of us from God, but Jesus took our sin upon himself when he died on the cross. His death and resurrection became the bridge to restoring our relationship with God. Jesus wants to give you new life that overflows with hope for eternal things. We can find true joy if we believe that Jesus is "the way, the truth, and the life" (John 14:6).

So let me ask you: What brings you joy? I hope that you look to Jesus today to find your true purpose and God-given identity and to experience the joy and peace he offers!

I pray that God, the source of hope,
will fill you completely with joy and peace
because you trust in him. Then you will
overflow with confident hope through
the power of the Holy Spirit.

ROMANS 15:13

Acknowledgments

I AM SO THANKFUL TO GOD for blessing me with such a joyful and beautiful life. I don't ever want to take for granted the amazing life I have been given, and I want to live out my days sharing God's joy with others!

Thank you to my parents, Bruce and Sherry, for encouraging me in all I've ever done and giving me a wonderful foundation and more support than I ever could have asked for. I love you both so much!

And thank you to my husband, Phil, who puts up with all my crazy, ever-changing ideas and dreams. I couldn't do any part of this beautiful life without you. Thank you for continuously loving me and our children just exactly the way each of us needs to be loved!

About the Author

LINDSEY BONNICE IS MARRIED to her high school sweetheart and is Mama to four beautiful children. Her family has been blessed by adoption, and she loves to share their journey whenever she has the chance. She lives on a miniature farm in the hills of northeastern Pennsylvania, where she's surrounded by cute, fluffy critters in a home painted in pastels and filled with lots of joy and whimsy!

More than anything, Lindsey loves taking pictures of her kids and animals. She also enjoys decorating, eating chocolate and sweets, and snuggling with her kiddos. Lindsey has been a professional photographer for more than fifteen years and is the author of *Libby and Pearl*, a children's book showcasing her beautiful images. She has been featured in many magazines, online publications, TV shows, and more.

One of Lindsey's biggest passions is being a children's designer. In 2014, she created the whimsical boutique-style Live Sweet Shop, a beautiful online site with gifts for the young and young at heart. Lindsey creates the products in partnership with local women, providing them with secure jobs, and donates part of the proceeds to families going through the adoption process. She is also a business coach who loves creating online content and supporting women in business.

Visit the whimsical world of

L*ive SWEET

Lindsey is the founder and creative behind Live Sweet Shop, a boutique that sells handmade whimsical gifts for the young and young at heart! Each piece is made with custom-designed pastel fabrics and is crafted by local artists and seamstresses. Lindsey launched Live Sweet Shop in 2015 and has been featuring her products in photos like these ever since!

Join the Facebook group "Live Sweet Loves" or follow us on Instagram (@livesweetshop) to learn all about Live Sweet, and shop for our products online at shoplivesweet.com!

CP1626